THE MAN ˅ YEARS IN THE BATH

by

A.F. Harrold

with eight illustrations by
Richard Ponsford

By the same author

Poetry
Logic And The Heart (Love Poems 1999-2003) (2004, *Two Rivers Press*)

Entertainment
Postcards From the Hedgehog (2007, *Two Rivers Press*)

First published in the UK in 2008 by

Quirkstandard's **Alternative**
79a Northumberland Avenue
Reading
Berkshire
RG2 7PT

www.afharrold.co.uk
www.quirkstandardsalternative.co.uk

Cover design and layout by Richard Lucas

ISBN-13: 978-0-9557081-0-7

Printed and bound by CPI Antony Rowe, Eastbourne

For David Yates,
a delight of a man whose imagination
has occasionally crossed paths with mine.

Acknowledgements

Some poems first appeared, sometimes in slightly different forms, on the A.F. Harrold CDs *Revels Without Applause* (2003) (*I Gave My Heart To A Sailor*), *Between A Yak And A Hard Plaice* (2005) (*Jam; Leonardo da Vinci; Sir Isaac Newton; The Edgar Degas Poem; I Went To A Fancy Dress Party; Kitchen Poem, #1; Aunt Mable; The Man Who Spent Years In The Bath; Testimony Of A Mediaeval Monk*), *An Englishman's Home Is His (Modestly Priced) Third Album* (2006) (*A Party At George Gershwin's; The Sitwell Song; Aunt Daisy*) and *Left Out Of The Left Field* (2006) (*Not Waving (At Trains); Story; Meditation On Dead Souls; Short Announcement By The Arles Town-Crier; Short Play Based On Shakespeare's* Julius Caesar; *A Sad Ballad, With A Bit Of Sunlight Here And There; Nikolai Gogol: How To Get Ahead In Literature*).

Water – A Short History and *Aunt Edith's Thirty-Ninth Birthday Island* were originally made available as parts of a pod-cast entitled *An Irregular Miscellany: A Collection of Lectures and Essays from the Annals of the Common University* (2006), still available on-line via www.podiobooks.com. (The latter was a footnote from the unpublished novel about pirates (among other things) *On The Trail Of The Treasure Of Teresa-Maria*.)

Contents

The Man Who Spent Years In The Bath

One day,
in June, I think it was,
a man decided to have a bath.

Up to that point he had shown no particular inclination towards
or love of unexpected behaviour,
in actual fact,
people said,
he was quite normal.

However,
to himself,
he had always wished there was time enough in the day for two baths,
each of, at least,
an hour's duration with hot water and warm towels waiting.

Usually he could make time only for a short one in the evening
before retiring
although his wife encouraged him to take showers
which saved water
and were hot and invigorating and quicker.

The beauty of the bath,
he would explain quietly,
is that it is **not** quicker or invigorating,
instead, he said,
it is slow and patient and laps gently
at the underside
of the imagination,
somewhere between waking and working,
somewhere off,
in brackets from life.

His wife usually ignored him and went out to work.

So, as I said,
one day in June,
several years ago now,
he ran a bath,
stripped off
and stepped in.

He has said that this bath was,
in origin,
no different to any other bath he'd run,
but somewhere after the first ten minutes
he realised
that a bridge had been charred,
something inside him had snapped a little
and his mind had been made up.

In the bath, he maintained,
he was able to think clearer and to write better and
    understand more.
Problems slipped away simply,
and for the first time in years poems bubbled up
through the water
into his half-closed eyes.

Great poems, small poems, free verse, sonnets,
limericks, clerihews, imitations, intimations,
all lined orderly into his inner eye.

He knew he was sitting at the wellspring
of some great aquifer
of verse,
in command of a unbidden body of beauty,
and he knew that such a find brought with it duties

and he set himself to recording his *oeuvre*.
But he found his paper simply pulped,
his ink dyed the water and stained the enamel,
his laptop short-circuited.

He dictated to his daughter
but she was uninterested
and quickly
grew bored with the exercise.

His son couldn't write.

His wife was too busy to listen for long.

He topped the water up,
draining a little out and tapping a little in.

New water for cold.

Hot water for old.

And he thought more.

Repeating his poems to himself he found them growing better,
he found verse spinning off into new poems,
into plays, into short stories, lyrical and fragile and laced
    with wit.

He kept fit by swimming lengths.

Repeating his work to himself
so as to not lose it before he could record it
he found new directions open before him.
His mind, drifting somewhere between waking and working,
was like a dove in the flood,

each time bringing home something in its beak,
something that contained a sign and a prayer and a dream
and a promise.

He got out very briefly each day,
when everyone was away,
to use the lavatory.

Repeating everything over and over in his head,
mumbling a little under his breath,
splashing a little with one hand or the other,
he discovered lost myths and forgotten fables,
he coxed for the Argonauts
and played cards with Cervantes,
he discovered corners of literature in which he could make a mark,
corners that he could whip the cobwebs from to uncover,
to uncover what…?
Well, he never knew until he tugged and then there it simply was.

Addicted to this bath, high on the creativity it inspired in him,
he didn't notice how long he had been there,
a month or two perhaps, he guessed,
but he wasn't concerned and his wife, who was at heart loving,
brought him his tea and would listen to his latest effort,
smile,
kiss him
and leave to watch Eastenders.

His daughter,
however,
who was at this time a teenager,
was less impressed with her father's predilection for submersion.

The first month or two it had seemed odd but novel.

After six months she had grown too embarrassed to bring friends
   home,
fearing that they would need to use the lavatory,
which, although not actually in the same room as the bath,
was in the room next door
and the walls were quite thin
and she didn't want them to hear her dad reciting to himself,
splashing happily,
scrubbing his back as he tested the sounds
and stresses
in some new villanelle or tectratys.

When the first anniversary of his getting in the bath occurred
his wife made him a cake,
his daughter bought him a Dictaphone
and his son joined the army.

The humidity in the bathroom warped the tape in the Dictaphone
but he appreciated the thought.

Recently he had discovered a talent for composing
one act verse tragedies
and could be heard upstairs
playing all the parts himself
in a variety of voices
interlaced with moans
and screams
and an occasional
final
sullen
death rattle.

Soon though he slipped into a light-hearted imagist period
which proved much less distracting
to those others who shared his house.

On his second anniversary his son came home on leave
and brought his new boyfriend with him.

The boyfriend happened to be a poet too
and spent much of his weekend's leave perched on the edge of
    the bath
swapping sonnets and ballads.

Other than on his wife's daily visits, with his dinner or tea,
no one had ever really listened to his poems before,
and certainly no one who actually understood the trials of being
a neglected and fractured artist.

His daughter left to go to university.

He stood on tiptoe
and waved from the open frosted window.

The calendar rolled on
and the water dipped down and topped up
and the hum of the extractor fan came on earlier in the afternoon
and outside,
somewhere,
the leaves where shifting to the ground
and it was a little over three years since he had stepped into the bath.

He stood up,
towelled himself dry,
sprinkled talcum powder over his pale, undulated skin
and slipped into a nice pair of cool
cotton
pyjamas.

His wife was surprised to find his lump
waiting for her
in their bed
when she came up after Newsnight.

She had heard the gurgling away
of the bathwater
through the pipes earlier
but had thought nothing of it, absently.

She welcomed him back with a kiss
and a hug
and switched off the light, saying, 'Mmm,
                                        something smells nice.'

'Yes dear,' he said, 'It's the talcum powder.'

The next morning, October the 14th,
he went into work and explained why he hadn't been in for a while.

When he came home that evening he sat with his wife
at the dinner table.

Since both the children had left home they were alone.

'It was nice to be a poet,'
he said,
'Those were beautiful songs I could hear
while I was in the bath.
And the stories were full of love
and meaning
and laughter.
I wish I could remember them now.'

He cried, just a tiny bit.

His wife looked at him and smiled.
'It's good to have you back,' she said,
'Maybe you'd like to share a shower.
                    I have poetry too.'

Jam

What are Jammie Dodgers dodging?
Presumably things that would otherwise lodge in
the jam in the middle or the biscuity bit.
I guess that's it.

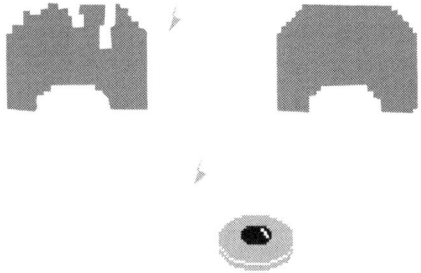

Not Waving (At Trains)

In poetry books, in libraries up and down the kingdom
poets have constructed poems about children in fields
delighting at the passing of the metal and glass monster,
roaring along, delightfully, childfully
                                        waving at trains.

But here's a caveman, in his cave, wrapped in the fur
of something he's killed himself, hunched by his hearth,
blowing the embers, fanning his fire,
                                        waving at flames.

Here's an old-fashioned schoolmaster, stood in his study,
boys quietly crying before him, signalling punishment,
smilingly choosing his weapon,
                                        waving at canes.

Then there's the hardboiled private eye or dick, gesturing
a party of prospective clients into his office,
                                        waving at dames.

And now here's a child who's been sadly locked in a toy shop,
trying to reach, through the night, the shelves out of his reach,
searching for novelty,
                                        waving at games.

Or Jesus, one day, is down on the beach when he notices
one of his Apostles coming back from a dip in the sea
heading up the wrong strip of sand (which all looks the same)
and spends a minute helpfully shouting and
                                        waving at James.

On a trip round a graveyard, on a long Sunday walk,
you'd show me stone after stone, and I remember you
reciting the dates,

                     waving at names.

The doctor, who as ever is short of time and patience and manners,
shows the nurse the patient suggesting the blood sample
be taken from here, gesturing vaguely

                     waving at veins.

And look, the trainee ornithologist spends his first day
out by the river excitedly ticking off herons and storks,
thanking each one with a sweep of his hat in his hand,
believing himself to be

                     waving at cranes.

And so, when the world throughout time
has been generous with and passionate about
so many things that almost sound the same
don't ever feel that you ought to restrict yourself
to standing in fields staring into the sky waving at planes
or over the hedge waving at trains
but revel in the positive multiplicity of things
you can begin to include

                     with the simplest of gestures.

A Party At George Gershwin's

The last time I saw George Gershwin
was in Crawley in '71 –
the party was simply perfection,
it was truly the acme of fun.
George Orwell was leant in one corner
and George de la Mare in another
(and in case anyone's wondering
that's Walter's less well known brother).

As George Eliot danced a fandango
Bernard Shaw stared hard at her bust
which jiggled about as his hand reached out
and she said 'Go on then George, if you must.'
But then George Martin put on a record
that he'd specially had brought along
and everyone raised their dark glasses
and squinted because of the sun

that shone so bright through the window,
which George Formby had polished all morning
whilst sharing lewd tales of the things he had seen
which he hoped would serve us as a warning.
Whatever they were (I forget now)
they were the most memorable thing of the night –
except for the food and Shaw in the nude
and the carpeting, weather and fight,

'cause George Foreman got angry quite early
and refused to join in with Charades
and 'though most of the company laughed at this
George Harrison took it quite hard
and grabbing whatever was handy
commenced to assault the dissenter

and had to be shot through a blow-dart-pipe
with a tranquillised scrap of polenta

but not before wounding George Foreman
by inserting an old telephone
(the type that had ear-piece and mouth-piece
and that stood proud on a table alone
in the hallway or bedroom or elsewhere,
which was not like the phones of today
which are made from the slightest of plastics
and that are constantly blowing away,

no this phone was a hardwood construction,
it was ebony, with wires like rope,
and required the aid of a woman
(with a voice like a young antelope)
to connect you to whom you were calling
(it had no dial to snag fingernails) –
and she'd say, 'Caller, go ahead, you're connected.'
in a purr that just never fails

to excite the masculine properties
of a gentleman using the phone
(in fact I've spent many long evenings
connecting, with her, on my own)).
So anyway, the phone was inserted
and George Foreman remained standing up
from then till the end of the party,
regularly raising his cup

and singing along with the sing-songs
and later on dancing till four

or five young men from the kitchens
carried Georges Simenon out to the door,
shouting coarse phrases in Belgian
which no one would deign to translate.
Santayana claimed it either too early
for language like that, or too late.

And so we were split down the middle
and the party just ended like that.
George Sanders looked bored in the hallway
as he tried to decide on which hat
either was his or would suit him
and then we filed on out to the street
and stood in the coolness awhile
remarking on how very neat

the stars were arranged in the sky there
and on how lovely it was to live
and Georges Pompidou opened his wallet
and gave away all he could give.
We hugged and embraced (a touch drunk)
and I believe, in retrospect, that we sang,
until blankly we looked at each other
as somewhere a telephone rang.

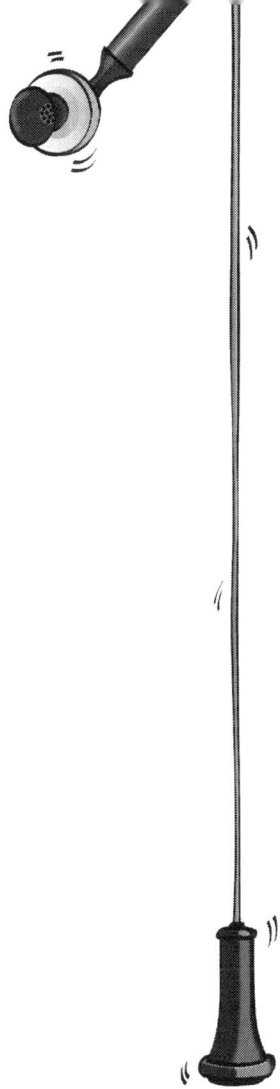

Story

I'm writing a novel about a virtuoso concert pianist, who, after years of being incensed, outraged and aggrieved by the unscripted percussive expectorations and incalculable and chronic bronchial contributions of English audiences, has his agent book him on a concert tour around the sanatoria of this fair country, where with a subtlety and an irony that can hardly be credited he waits for the tubercular inhabitants' hacking, coughing and retching to reach a majestic crescendo of power and emotion, whereupon he interjects an unwanted Bach fugue.

So far, few publishers have answered my request for a large advance.

Leonardo da Vinci

When Leonardo da Vinci
invented the lever
and also the winch he
was stuck in Geneva.

He was locked in a hotel
by a Prince who repented
his dictate that no tel-
ephones be invented.

A small helicopter
got drawn on a hanky.
He checked the dioptre
but still got quite cranky

when he noticed his photos
had all come out sepia.
But the Prince had no toes
which da Vinci found creepier.

So to make things nicer
he phoned out to Pisa,
said, 'Send the Mona Lisa
or, if not, the Mona Lisa.'

Whichever, they sent it,
but da Vinci weren't happy,
'cause the Post Office bent it
and now it looked crappy.

Sir Isaac Newton

Isaac Newton invented gravity
one afternoon in the 17th century
before he did this life had been
very interesting indeed:

when for example an apple
that had been happily growing on a tree let go
it would just hang there in the air
bobbing to and fro;

or when a flying fish
leapt out of the water
in order
to glide above the deck of a ship
it would, more often than not,
carry on upwards
until the friction of the air
slowed its momentum to zero
at which point it would become prey
for a wandering wandering albatross;

and when, in 1066, William the Conqueror
decided to invade England
he stood and mingled
on the hard French shingle
with 16,000 of his men,
who, at his signal ran towards the sea,
jumping into the air at the last moment
and flying across the waves
towards the English coast –

when they were halfway across
William instructed his men to flap

once in a upwards direction
thus making the necessary course correction
to their angle of attack
and as we know from our history books
William, and his Normans, never looked back.

But what, I hear you ask,
kept the sea in its place?
Well that's quite simple,
it was just a rather large and intricate layer of lace
that was made many centuries before
when the nations decided in-between some war
or other that it would be a good idea
to keep the water near the ground
instead of letting it float around
in pointless spheres
as it had done for years,

because sometimes someone wanted a drink
and would turn around only to find
that all the water had drifted away into Outer Space, again,

hence the multi-national effort on the lace and then

one afternoon, in the late 17th century,
when Isaac Newton was sat beneath a tree,
grasping the grass to stop himself from drifting free,
he saw an apple detach itself from the branch
and fall towards his head as a chance
gust of wind blew from behind
and this put the thought into his mind
that if, in general, as a rule, things fell down
everything would be much easier all round

and so he spent several years in his laboratory
where he experimented with alchemy
and mystical mathematical formulations from the East
until eventually he came up with something that seemed ideal, at least.

It was a small wooden box, labelled 'Gravity' with a button on the top
and no way to ever turn it off or stop
and he showed it to the King and to the Royal Society
and they all said 'Go on then Isaac press the button,'
and he did and watched as the looks sank on everyone's faces
because, hitherto, it was true, the flesh there had been weightless
and the king slumped in his throne, emitting a groan,
and from outside came the thump thump thud
as citizens and scholars fell from the sky into the mud
along with fruit of various descriptions
and birds who had not quite learnt how to fly under the new conditions
imposed by Newton's box
and finally there was a series of splats
and a few voluminous plops
as a small red, sly fox
and the entire Quorn
collapsed in a bloody heap on the lawn.

And although, it was admitted, the start was a bit sticky
people had a general feeling that Newton's gravity
would be a good idea in the long run
and in fact made possible all sorts of fun
such as hang-gliding
and that thing at the funfair where you're pinned to the wall
and the floor falls away,
and people were heard to say
that it was shame that Newton never got to see his dream fulfilled
since he hadn't looked up before he turned it on and was, sadly, by
    falling courtiers killed.

Water – A Short History

Before Christopher Columbus sailed for the East by going West, Europe was a very different place. For example, Germany was just that little bit further to the south and people were reluctant to say 'Bless You' when one sneezed for fear of the Inquisition. It was during the age of rapid and unprecedented exploration that followed his historic voyage that, for example, many nowadays commonplace foodstuffs were placed for the first time upon the plates of noblemen and commoners alike in the Old World. The potato. Tobacco. Tomatoes. Chocolate, coffee and sweetcorn, but the one discovery that changed the entire face of Western Civilization more than any other was water, or as contemporary manuscripts have it 'walter'.

In 1595 Walter Veranputti, an Italian cobbler by trade, was in debt. His cobbles were too short for the trends of the time and didn't speak English which estranged them from the Court, who mostly only spoke French. Consequently he had fallen out of favour with Queen Elizabeth who, it was widely believed, was happy to support struggling but solvent artists and he had unsurprisingly fallen into a desperate stupor. Whilst in this stupor he lost his home, his livelihood, his manlihood and his ridinghood to the moneylenders. Penniless, bereft of high-level support and unwilling to go home to his mother in Basingstoke, Veranputti stowed away on the first ship he saw moored in the docks. He took with him his final crust of bread and his favourite cobble.

Three weeks later, and somewhere in the mid-Atlantic, Veranputti declared his presence to the Captain, hoping to simply be put to work and given something, however small, to eat. (His crust of bread being almost finished.) The Captain, however, was an honest and practical man and explained that he had provisioned the ship with exactly the amount of food needed to feed exactly the number of men on board for exactly the length of time they'd be at sea for and not a sausage more. (Actually there were no sausages on board at all, for 1595 had been a particularly bad winter for the sausage growers of the south-coast and only imported sausages were on the market and only then at exorbitant prices.) The Captain laboriously explained that were Veranputti to eat of their stores he would be depriving another member of the crew of their loaf of bread or potato cigarette, and that, clearly, wouldn't be cricket, which is, in fact, some sort of ball game or insect.

However, an idea floated to the surface of the Captain's mind mere moments later. He had found, after several weeks of voyaging, that authority and responsibility had settled uncomfortably on his shoulders. If Veranputti would take over his role as Captain and allowed him, the Captain, to take over Veranputti's role as stowaway, with the last crumbs of Veranputti's loaf of bread, then there would be no imbalance in the provisions or crew numbers and he, the Captain, would get a chance to put his feet up. A little confused at the Captain's plan Veranputti swiftly agreed and the two men swapped clothes, addresses and several small but not necessarily inconsequential diseases.

Captain Veranputti's first order as captain was to search the ship for stowaways and to cast them overboard as an example to any would-be stowaways in the area. He became a harsh but fair captain and few people crossed him twice, which only goes to show that stern discipline never goes astray. Which isn't to say that stern discipline never goads a stray. Obviously.

Naval provisions in this era consisted of the juice of one lime per man per day, one dry nautical biscuit per man per day, one strip of salted pork per man per day, followed by crackers, cheese and a selection of sweets from the trolley. It was a hard regime for very fat people or anyone with a dislike for fruit, biscuits or meat, made liveable only by the single glass of whiskey each man was allowed twice before he retired to his quarters for the evening, which were sometimes shared between as few as twenty-two sailors. Nobody pretended it was an easy life but if you treated it with respect and an open eye then you might get to die at home, on the shore, bitterly regretting every moment of it, instead, of course, of dying at sea feeling exactly the same way.

Eventually, after several more weeks, Veranputti set foot on that part of the American coastline that in later years remained part of the American coastline, but which at this time was part of India. Here, after planting the flag of Good Queen Bess and having himself photographed beside it by a fortuitously passing local entrepreneur, he proceeded to visit several Irish theme bars and collapse in the gutter shortly before midday.

It was here, three days later, that Walter Veranputti made the startling discovery that would ensure his name became a household one. He looked up thickly at the low and ominous rumbling above him and ran through a list of possible sources in his head. Volcano? Not visibly. Earthquake? The earth wasn't quaking. Stampede? Didn't smell like it. Then the miraculous occurred, then the revelatory, the event that changed all history, that set the course of future discoveries, of future lives – something landed on his forehead.

It felt as if a spot had burst somewhere above his eyes and he wrinkled his brow. It was a sudden feeling of being tapped, as if by a finger or stick perhaps, and then a residual moistness, but when he raised his finger there was no pus only something transparent, something that coated his finger with a glimmer of reflectivity. It was magic, he thought, but then another spot popped into being on his cheek and then on the back of his hand, each of them traceless and see-through.

As he slowly moved his attention from himself to the world around him he could see the same sourceless spots bursting into being on the soil, on the pavement, on the small dog by his side. And looking up he could make out faint traces in sky, silvery lines into the heavens, and his face was covered with what now he recognised to be a gift from the New World Gods. He cupped his hands and slowly they filled with the cold, slimy, wholly transparent substance. It slipped from between his fingers, but his fleshy bowl filled faster than it emptied, and soon he was able to put it to his lips and sip the nectar. There was a distant blue flash that illuminated the skyline and the night and there was more rumbling from all around. As he swallowed he noted the texture, thinner than saliva; its taste, softer than whiskey; and its coolness, refreshing in the humidity of the night.

Within the week Veranputti had named his discovery after himself and had filled twelve large tar-sealed barrels with it. With these twelve barrels of walter he planned to make his fortune, indeed to remake his fortune in London, never forgetting for one moment that short cobbles are what cobbling is really all about – true style is timeless and unconstrained by fashion. The uses of this liquid, he theorised, were almost limitless. It could be rubbed onto the body and with the use of a cloth or small soft stone could be used to remove caked dirt; it could be drunk without the age old problem of subsequently falling down; it could be eaten if mixed with the dry nautical biscuits from the ship's hold. In fact, not only did it improve the texture of the biscuits but it also floated the little weevils and maggots to the surface of the walter, which could then simply be scooped off and fried up elsewhere, which meant, in practice, that the more squeamish members of society no longer had a good reason for not wanting to serve Her Majesty in the Royal Navy. But this wasn't all, Veranputti calculated that walter could be used to make dry stone walls wet, to make dry white wine more appetising and most importantly of all it could be used to float candles. This, he realised, may well enrage certain members of the sconce making guilds but would, on the whole, be much more romantic.

And so it was on a cold June morning that Veranputti sailed into Portsmouth with twelve sealed barrels in the hold and a song in his heart. It wasn't a very good song admittedly, but Veranputti had never pretended to be a songwriter and figured that once he'd made his fortune (again), by selling the secret of walter, walter itself and the madrigal rights to his story, he'd be able to hire a professional songwriter to write him a new, more sophisticated song which made use of syncopation and a humorous chorus.

So it was, as we've almost said before, on a cold July morning that Veranputti strode into the Court of Queen Elizabeth I with his unfashionably short cobbles standing proud, his dirty travel-worn ruff hanging limp and the first twelve barrels of walter ever seen in the Old World.

The Queen declared that she much preferred Raleigh's potatoes and the rest, as they say, is history.

Jubilate Balneis – Rejoice In The Bath

Let Poseidon preserve and protect me in the tub:
puff suds from my eyes and make my wrinkles merry;
keep thorny coral away and let sleeping sharks lie;
prevent the plug from popping prematurely.

For a bath is a boat, with the water on the inside.
For a bath brings the peace of the open sea, but warmer.
For a bath is a solitary place of solitude in a busy world.

Let the numerous Nereids keep cold enamel at bay
and guide treacherous bars of soap from underfoot;
ensure the taps are turnable by toes, that the water
falls piping hot from the faucet: let it steam the mirror.

For a bath is a boat, with the water on the inside.
For few wars have ever been started from a bath.
For great ideas are discovered there.

Lord Neptune, by your power prevent the miserly bath:
baths lasting less than an hour; baths where nipples sit
above the water line; baths over which a clock ticks.
Soak the clocks, Lord Neptune, and sponge the miser.

For a bath is a boat, with the water on the inside.
For the radio can be heard there, and books can be read.
For the telephone should not reach you.

Let God save those in peril in the bath: the elderly,
the infirm, the babes-in-arms – float them and ease them,
bubble around them and buoy them up, brace them
in your warm water embrace: keep them safe, always.

For a bath is a boat, with the water on the inside.
For water is a slow element, a long low element.
For the ancients knew of the bath.

Lake, loch, mere, tarn, hammer-pond, mill-pond, pool:
let these be a place in every house, hot and private.
Let those who spy on the bath, who knock on the door,
who interrupt the retreat be devoured by their own dogs.

For a bath is a boat, with the water on the inside.
For everyone should respectfully hide away and roughly soap.
For it is truly next to godliness.

Let the Great First Sea Lord see that I safely survive to see
the far shore of towels, the heaped dunes of towelling;
let me doze contentedly between chapters, the hum
of pipework playing its lapadaisical lullaby. Let it lull me.

For a bath is a boat, with the water on the inside.
For every submergement is a journey out of the day-to-day.
For the bather-explorer is pink and blessed.

Poseidon, Neptune, Triton have pity on those people
who have shower-rooms, with no space for a bathtub.
It is truly said 'into every life a little rain will fall'.
May they visit hotels and spas and often and soon.

For a bath is a boat, with the water on the inside.
For a world of baths is a joyous place of distant splashing.
For even cats will perch on the bath rim, approving the idea.

Old Men of the Sea, and Goddesses of the Foam,
when my day comes take me to you. Let me slip
into long death in the bath, in the warm, like sleep.
Take me like Marat or Seneca, but with less fuss.

For a bath is a boat, with the water on the inside.
For the longest journeys have always happened there.
For it is dark outside the dripping window.

Meditation On Dead Souls

I was stuck in a room with a bunch of Russian scholars.
From a mile away you could have heard the hollers
as they shouted and they raged at the top of their voices
berating one another and their tastes and their choices.

One of them liked Tolstoy but one of them did not.
One of them was happy Mayakovski had been shot.
One of them rated Goncharev above the normal rabble
(there were other names I didn't know which would score equally
    well in Scrabble).

One of them said 'Chekhov is the only one who'll last.'
Another man looked gloomy saying 'Chekhov goes too fast.'
Other constant disagreements of a similar hue and ilk
seemed to be for these gentlemen like water, bread and milk,

and there was only one thing to which they'd all consent,
that stopped them from fighting and getting broke and bent
and that was that *The Overcoat* is a jolly good short story
and the man who wrote the thing deserves unending literary glory –

it was Gogol á gogo, Gogol á gogo, Gogol á gogo, it that room,
it was Gogol á gogo, Gogol á gogo, Gogol á gogo, go go Gogol!

Put Gogol into Google and you get a million sites,
enough to keep a Russophile awake a thousand nights.
Gogol probably pranced around in a furry hat and tights
but I haven't done the research so that bit might be wrong.

The Edgar Degas Poem

Edgar was not what you'd call loquacious.
His conversation was noted to be fairly spacious.
If ever asked a question he might give a reply
or he might gaze up at the clouds in the sky.

He was handsome enough if not really vivacious.
He grew himself a beard to look a little sagacious.
But the friends that he had liked him anyway
even if he rarely came out to play –

'cause Edgar could paint, could paint, could paint,
yes, Edgar could paint you a picture.

He'd whip out his pastels and make a quick sketch
of some young ballerina girls having a stretch
or some blokes riding horses just prior to racing
and he was so good it didn't matter which way they were facing –

'cause Edgar could paint, could paint, could paint,
yes, Edgar could paint you a picture.

He'd invite a lady round to do some ablutions
and remain just a staid as a dozen Confucians
rubbing his pastel on a big bit of paper
and chuckling to himself at this marvellous caper.

And when his friends called, said 'Ed come down the pub!'
he'd look at his model, give his chin a rub,
and say 'Well I could do that or I could stay here,'
and as he made his decision he rubbed his ear

which he wouldn't've been able to do had he been Vincent van Gogh.

The Don Miguel de Cervantes Poem

My name is Cervantes,
I come from Madrid,
I don't write books now
but you know once I did.

A Poem About King Cnut And His Chief Advisor

Godwin's king, in Godwin's eyes,
lost God's highest given right
to being king
by paddling.

Short Announcement By The Arles Town-Crier

Earless! Earless!

FRANCE

(Arles is 'ere)

Aunt Edith's Thirty-Ninth Birthday Island

There has been some confusion as to the provenance of this particular island's name, especially considering the proximity of it (within forty miles) to Aunt Edith's Fortieth Birthday Island. Sometimes people, who clearly lack basic historical knowledge, have asked where the other thirty-eight Aunt Edith's Birthday islands are, assuming them to be part of a chain of sequentially numbered landmasses. To call this question ignorant is to be justifiably rude to the questioner, but is not really acceptable behaviour in polite company.

Upon inspection, however, the matter is in fact absolutely simple and straightforward. There are only two islands named for the birthdays of Aunt Edith, and they are named thusly as a part of a great nautical tradition.

In the first days of exploration explorers would, as a general rule, name the first place they discovered after their Monarch, the second place after themselves and the third place after their First Mate. Lands discovered after that were named by working sequentially down through the ranks, starting maybe with the Lad-in-the-Crow's-Nest followed by the Ship's Doctor, then the Ship's Natural Philosopher and so on. But a limit was discovered as to how many crew members could have islands named after them, because, it is an inescapable truth that the number of crew on board any particular ship must always be finite.

Once all those names had been exhausted Captains would often look to the Ship's Calendar and name the islands after the particular day on which they were encountered, hence Tuesday Island in the East Indies, Wednesday Island in the South Atlantic and La Isla Dominga in the Bay of Biscay. After they had run through the days of the week in all the languages they knew they tended to look into the corners of the calendar where Bank Holidays and Saint's Days were listed. In this way St. Lucia (West Indies) and the Old Man of St. Vitus (North Sea) were named, along with Christmas and Easter Islands and the less well-known National Egg Awareness Day Island located a few miles north of Svalbard.

But this had its limits too, even on board those ships with Roman Catholic Calendars filled with their innumerable Saints. Even utilising additional calendars, say Mohammaden or Jewish ones, only helped provide a further finite number of extra names, Passover Island (Indian Ocean) and the Ramadan Rocks (The Wash) being the best known examples.

It was following this period of exploration that the two Aunt Edith's Birthday islands were discovered and named. The first, the Thirty-Ninth, was found in 1763 and named after the Captain's Cabin Boy's Aunt's birthday which the Cabin Boy had only just remembered. Since he'd forgotten to send her a card, and since it was now too late to do so, and he was feeling quite bad about it, the crew decided to throw her a little party, even though she was many thousands of miles away and, as luck would have it, had died the previous spring when a freak waterspout swept several dozen Maiden Aunts up from Oxford Circus and rained them inexplicably over the North Sea some hours later. (To be fair, it was only inexplicable to the fish, who watched bemused, never having seen a Maiden Aunt in such deep water before.)

After the party they decided to stay on for a few weeks since the island was glorious, bountiful and utterly beautiful. They restocked their fresh water butts and their larders and sat underneath the palm trees eating fresh fruit. Unfortunately this gave them the most dreadful upset stomachs and the whole character of the island changed almost overnight. They were incapacitated for some months and when most of the crew eventually felt well enough to sail away they spent several months cruising in circles just a few miles off the coast, since the man who was in charge of the wheel had to keep nipping off to the heads (nautical toilets).

It was in this way that it took them a whole year to cross the forty mile stretch of water in-between the two islands and it was purely by chance that they arrived at the second of the Aunt Edith's Birthday islands on exactly the same date as they had the previous one. Nobody had any better suggestions and a tradition was a tradition and so the appellation was duly noted on the charts.

Similar misfortune beset the crew as they left this island and once again it took them exactly an entire year to reach their next undiscovered port of call. This time however they sailed around it a few times before landing just in order to give someone else a chance at providing the name. This time it fell to the Bosun's Aunt to provide it, and so in 1765 Aunt Edith (Brown)'s Birthday Island filled another blank in the world's gazetteer.

Once all the important days of the calendar and of people's personal lives had been used up, however, explorers kept on discovering islands and the islands kept on demanding names.

This penultimate and fairly short-lived phase of island naming resulted in some inspired places being found, places such as Chair Island and Table Island (members of the Maldives), Deck Island and Scrubbing Brush Island (off the coast of Newfoundland), Map Island and Compass Island (South-West Pacific), and towards the end Shirt Island, Hat Island and Trousers Island (eventually amalgamated as the Isle of Dogs).

Once the nomenclature of all the articles that the sailors could spy on their ships had been used up they sailed on desperately hoping to avoid finding any new islands, but they did find them and they kept on finding them, because the oceans are so very large and the islands are so numerously scattered across them.

Out of a growing sense of despair it was then that one enterprising young First Mate suggested to his Captain that perhaps they might ask the people who lived on the islands they found what they called them and just write that down on the charts. The Captain stared blankly at his First Mate for a few moments before asking him to explain it again.

It just didn't seem right somehow, the Captain thought, but these were desperate times, he had to admit, and they called for some desperate measures to be taken.

The first island they landed on they discovered, when a native was interrogated, was called by a name which, in the native tongue, sounded almost exactly like 'Great Britain.' The Captain pointed out to his First Mate that this was just the sort of problem that arose when you trusted natives to do anything and explained to his crew that, as far as he was aware, that name was already in use and although he didn't blame the natives (which was a lie) for having come up with a name phonetically the same (since, after all, it did have a good ring to it), although clearly ontologically dissimilar, they'd have to come up with something else themselves.

There was a groan of exhaustion from the assembled crew who had already used up all the names they could think of and mutters of dissension were heard until a young gunner pointed over the bulwark at his mother who was waving at him and remarked that it looked very much as if they'd just arrived home in the very same Portsmouth they'd sailed away from seventeen years before.

The Captain apologised, rather half-heartedly, to the 'native' he had interrogated, suggested he improve his accent, which upon close inspection had simply proved to be a bit common, and let him go.

I Gave My Heart To A Sailor *(an Edwardian song)*

I gave my heart to a sailor who I met on the shore of the sea.
He held my hand and spoke soft words and gazed so tenderly.
   He walked me back to my boarding house
   and I was as quiet as very little mouse.
all shy was I as we kissed good night but he was as shy as me.

We met the next day by the pedalo pond and then we went to the zoo.
We shared ice creams upon the prom, then our beach towels we did strew.
   Our sandwiches were filled with sand,
   I almost wept when he took my hand
and gazed in my eyes and stroked my hair and said 'Darling, I love you.

At teatime I nibbled just the corner of a cake and I sipped a very tiny cup.
Mater noticed how I didn't touch the toast and she asked if
  anything was up?
   To answer her I could not do
   for she'd never had a sailor saying 'I love you' –
so I smiled to myself and just kept mum and sipped another teensy sup.

de dum de dum de dum de dum de dum diddle ei de doh

That evening we went out to a dance and we had the most delightful twirl.
Then he made me drink some fortified wine which sent my head all awhirl.
   When I awoke he had gone
   and I found my frock had been undone –
and it seems he's not so much a girl in every port as some port in
  every girl.

de dum de dum de dum de dum de dum diddle ei de doh

Now I know I'll never trust a man again as they all seem the same to me –
whether they're born in the áir, on land or especially out at sea –
   there's just one thing upon their mind
   and when it's done they're hard to find –
but still there's a part in my foolish heart that believes he really did
   love me –
but oh!, there's a part of my foolish heart that believes he really does
   love me.

I Went To A Fancy Dress Party

I went to a fancy dress party
dressed as a fireman.

On the way I helped an old lady's cat
out of a tree,

I used a handy set of wire cutters
to free an infant whose hand had become stuck
in some chain-link fencing

and I advised a small group
of office workers
which particular extinguisher
should be used on which particular fire.

When I got to the party
I was told it was a false alarm,
that there was no fire there
and that no one was stuck, flooded
or in any way in need of my help at all.

'Well,' I said, 'It's better safe than burning,'
and went back to the Fire Station
where I had a sandwich
and a game of cards with some real firemen.

After a while one of them noticed that my axe
was made of cardboard
and that I had painted a washing-up bowl yellow
and put it on my head.

I explained that I had been meaning to go to a fancy dress party
but that they hadn't needed me after all

and one of the firemen said that that had happened to him
just the weekend before and he'd had to spend the evening
in a convent
which had been a bit of an eye-opener,
he blushed in remembrance.

When our shift finished I filled in my time sheet
and one of the fireman gave me a ride home
on the back of his motorbike.

A Christmas Poem

When my Great Aunt Bertha,
who was a quaker, read in the papers
of how their boys and our boys all gave it up,
put them down and climbed over the top
to kick the patched leather ball
between barbed wire and crater rims,
between the two straight dark ditches they lived in,
she took it upon herself to head down to Woolworth's
and buy up all the marked down boxes of Christmas cards
lolling on the January shelves.

She spent her war years licking stamps,
inking addresses,
printing xmas messages in one of any number of different languages,
as appropriate,
signing her love
and visiting the pillarbox at the head of her road.
Sacks of the things went at once,
whole stretches of trench filled with spade-handled robins,
holly, magi, stockings and snow.
The babe of peace arrived in his manger,
in the stable,
in March, in April, in May,
ceaselessly,
year on year.

If there had been no calendars,
no officers, no orders,
no today's or yesterday's newspaper in the mess,
in the trench,
in the soldier's letter from home,
then her plan may have worked,
assuming the other side were equally ill-equipped

and open-mindedly eager to clutch peace as it passed.
But
no one was stupid enough to think it might be Christmas
every day,
no one was fooled by her hand,
and besides, the ball
needed pumping
and a puncture repair kit.
Great Aunt Bertha.

Aunt Daisy

Maiden aunt Daisy
was romantically lazy.
She never got bowled over
or rolled in the clover.

Aunt Mable, The 19th Century
Linguistic Freethinker Of Our Family

Auntie Mable
thought the fable
about Babel
in the Bible
to be unreliable.

The Sitwell Song

I sat down with several Sitwells
to a splendid and sumptuous supper.
Osbert was nowhere nearby
because he'd gone out to buy butter.
After an hour I feared for him so
and thought he had come a cropper,
but Edith remarked 'Don't worry, my boy,
he's a very meticulous shopper.
   A very meticulous shopper, indeed,
   a very meticulous shopper.'

Now, the Queen of Denmark was holding forth
on a subject close to her heart,
'To be nude is not rude in the land of my birth
in fact it's akin to an art,' she said.
Edith was the first to make an attempt
to put Her Highness at her ease
by removing her earrings and then all her clothes
in an angular sort of striptease.
   An angular sort of striptease, indeed,
   an angular sort of striptease.

Sacheveral stood and slapped at his side,
'Edith,' he said. 'Oh Edith,' he cried,
'Please have some decorum, let modesty linger.'
But Edith just turned and gave him the finger.
   Gave him the finger indeed, she did,
   gave him the finger indeed.

A snigger was heard from the end of the table
where Sir Winston Churchill sat.
He applauded at Edith's tenacity
and slowly removed his hat.

He took off his coat and took off his tie,
his trousers, his shirt and his bra
and sat there, a great pink pile of flesh,
a-puffing away his cigar.
    Puffing away his cigar, indeed,
    a-puffing away his cigar.

Sacheveral stood no longer for this
and out of room he strode,
grabbing his hat from the hallway hook
and blustering into the road.
All eyes at the table turned to me
(I felt duty and honour bound)
and quickly each article warming my corpse
slowly slipped to the ground.
    Slowly slipped to the ground, they did,
    slowly slipped to the ground.

The meal went ahead as only meals do
and no one was scalded or bitten,
and Edith was pointing out all sorts of things
that possibly someone had written.
Noël Coward was giving a lecture that night
on certain Peruvian tribes
who give access to rituals of bongo delight
for particularly moderate bribes.
    For particularly moderate bribes, indeed,
    for particularly moderate bribes.

The Queen of Denmark was raising her voice
and her arms and her chest and our eyes,
and speaking aloud of the uses of forks
we heard a loud cry of surprise.

From the doorway resounded a tremulous voice
which Edith was quick to place,
'Oh, Osbert!' she cried. 'Oh, Osbert my love!
If you'd look at the look on your face.
 If you'd look at the look on your face, indeed,
 if you'd look at the look on your face.'

Osbert placed the butter into the tray
(wonderfully set aside for this use)
and grabbing young Edith in both of his hands
he whittled a little excuse
explaining the lengths to which he had gone
to purchase the purchase he'd bought
from a swarthy gent of foreign persuasion
he'd met outside Bow Street Court.
 He'd met outside Bow Street Court, indeed,
 he'd met outside Bow Street Court.

Patrick Moore waved a hand high in the air
(well as high as young Patrick could reach)
and signalling frantically looked to the moon
which hung in the sky like a peach
(like a peach of particularly pale colouring
from which half was segmented away,
but all the same like a fruit which cannot be seen
by the light of the brightness of day.
 By the light of the brightness of day, not at all,
 by the light of the brightness of day).

And we noticed perched in the lunar sphere
a visage both dreadful and grim.
George Bernard Shaw chuckled and said
if you squinted it looked just like him.

Poor Moore took offence at such a poor jest
and challenged old Shaw to a duel.
So into the snow the both of them strode
armed each with a handful of gruel.
  Armed with a handful of gruel, they were,
  armed each with a handful of gruel.

Shaw threw at Moore just as Moore threw at Shaw
and gruel mixed between in the air.
With a terrible wail there arose a small gale
and the gruel missed both parts of the pair.
Shaw was sore shamed and Moore was the same
as each nude in the snow they stood –
vast islands of men with such space in-between.
The Queen giggled, 'Oh boys that was good.'
  She giggled, 'Oh, boys that was good, indeed,'
  she giggled, 'Oh boys that was good.'

Placated somewhat by the Queen's lack of wrath
the two men shook hands in the garden
but George Bernard Shaw let out a small roar
and resolutely refused to say pardon.
The atmosphere suffered, it's honest to say,
as George broke his wind once more.
Noël Coward just rose, uptilting his nose,
'Reminds one a bit of Roquefort,' he said.
  'Reminds one a bit of Roquefort, dear boy,
  reminds me a bit of Roquefort.'

Well, we all went inside. Desert had arrived –
we tucked into the trifle with relish
(a strange combination, caused quite a sensation
from Cissbury Ring to Mellish),

and after cigars our various cars
arrived one by one at the door.
Edith helped us out and fastened our belts
and we saw one another no more.

Now when it's cold in December I like to remember
the picture of George Bernard Shaw
standing out in the garden (no trace of a hard-on)
stark naked with young Patrick Moore –
for it's something to savour, no expense for the flavour
is shirked, as I've mentioned before
though we all went our ways I remember the days
and the nights of old '34.

I remember the days and all of the nights
   of the winter of old '34.
   Of the winter of old '34, indeed,
   of the winter of old '34.

   Of the winter of old '34, indeed,
   of the winter of old '34.

Kitchen Poem, #1

If you can't stand the heat
get in the fridge.

Shark Poem

If you believe the fact that in the shark
his bite being (really) much worse than his bark
doesn't disqualify him from being a good pet,
tell that, I suggest, to the one-armed vet.

A Sad Ballad, With A Bit Of Sunlight Here And There

I remember it as if it were yesterday,
the experience I'm about to relate.
It happened to me yesterday, as
I stood on my own by the gate.
I was leaning there watching the sun go down,
as I am wont to do,
when I thought I saw a lady pass by
who looked a lot like you.

This was somewhat unexpected you know,
you being so frightfully dead,
as is the usual consequence of
the body being clove from the head –
as happened to you three summers ago,
walking out on the lawn;
when our small son Sam shouted out, 'Daddy,
Mummy has upped and gone.'

Well I rushed to the garden, surprisingly quick
for a man of my height and girth,
and after I stooped to regain my breath your head
thudded down to the earth
with a splash where the blood of your life on the grass
of your home had formed a small pool
and in front of my eyes your body, still balancing
upright, was starting to cool.

Then Sam turned to me and he said, 'Dear Papa,
will Mater be all right for dinner?'
And I had to be honest with the poor darling boy,
'It's time for Mama to grow thinner,
and whither away and turn into dust
and be food for the grubs that would munch

on the flesh that we give to the sod with a death
that occurs so soon after lunch.'

For then, you remember, it was barely past two
and our luncheon had no time to settle
and you were taking a simple breath of fresh air,
which you said would be aiding your fettle
to be fine as is dandy, and I had retired
to the drawing room with a new pencil
and two sheets of paper to sketch out some visions
I'd had of a brand new utensil

(but not a normal or common or garden utensil,
no, an item of function and beauty
that would aid every man, and elderly gent,
in our Empire to fulfil his duty:
viz. being the finest, most upstanding subject
the Queen could desire to rule,
and all for the modest expense I would charge
to purchase my specialised tool).

But my sketch never made its way onto the page
because just then I heard the boy shout
and he'd never cried wolf, so I trusted his voice,
(enough follow it out)
and you were dead, oh my love, you were headless and dead
and your dress was no longer white,
and I held the small hand of our son in my hand
for I thought it would make things all right –

a bit of male bonding in the face of the tragic
and indeed we soon became friends,
and he shares in my wisdom and I share in his youth,
which is perfect for spotting new trends,
and we've designed, in my study, some marvellous things

that we've sold far and wide to the people
like a new sort of string and a cosy for vicars
to permanently place on their steeple.

So, three years have passed by in haze of production,
you'd be proud that we haven't stood still.
I've not married again although I've moved in
with the twins, Brian and Bill,
and they see to my needs and feed me and clothe me
and make sure I don't work too hard
and they insist every evening after repast
that we take a quick stroll round the yard.

And indeed it was after yesterday's stroll
that I leant on the gate in the dusk
and I caught the faint hint of a scent on the breeze
that was cinnamon mingled with musk
and that lady passed by, looking like you,
and my heart became empty with loss
and I shed a small tear, before going inside
for my usual post-prandial floss.

Two Intimations Of Mortality

Being interred
        should be deferred.
Being cremated
        is overrated.

Short Play Based On Shakespeare's *Julius Caesar*

Brutus: Hail Caesar. What should I call my newest short composition written for the piano that's designed as an exercise or to exploit technical virtuosity?

Caesar: Étude, Bruté.

A Bath Poem

If there's a fire in the house
don't scream and run and shout
just sit tight in the bath
and splash it all about.

Nikolai Gogol: *How To Get Ahead In Literature*

Nicko hitchhiked his way across the Ukraine
by lorry, bus, coach, car and train –
he worked for a week in a smoky little bar,
saving rouble notes inside his panties and his bra.
When he'd saved enough he bought a Smith Corona
that he'd seen in the free ads (only one careful owner)
and *clank clank* went the keys in the dark Russian night,
and as he banged away he knew to write was right.

He sold his first short story to Pravda for a fiver.
He said in a later interview he'd never felt aliver.
But he still stripped for money in a bar every day
and when he got home he'd bang the night away.
His second story was mentioned in a St Petersburg Salon
by very posh young women with very posh clothes on
and word crept to the Tsar about Nikolai's fine talents
and even he wanted to meet this new literary gallant –

and it looked like no more go-go bars for Nikolai Gogol,
no more watching sweaty men who've merely come to ogle
Nikolai Gogol.

So one evening Nicko ventured to society's upper stratum
(he was introduced as Google which required an erratum).
He sipped a fine red claret and he nibbled some ryvita
(he declined food more substantial saying he was never a big eater).
He tried to talk of stories and of literary devices
but a messenger rushed in for the Tsar with news of a crisis:
the serfs sought emancipation and they wanted it right now
and they were willing to uprise for it... the Italian ambassador said
　'ciao'.

The Tsar turned to Gogol and said 'Just tell me what you want
any sort of favour, any wishes I will grant,
if you'd use your magic word-wise tongue to disabuse the serfs
of their notions of equality, really show them what they're worth.'
So Gogol told the Tsar that he'd quite like a new coat
and if it wasn't too much trouble just a quick go in his boat,
and then he strode to the square where the serfs all had gathered
and he spoke very eloquently about things that really mattered.

His speech was very mighty, his speech was very fine,
the points he produced were apposite and it wasn't a long time
before the serfs were throwing fruit that was the other side of fresh
and all Nikolai's clothes got mucky and a bit of a mess.
So he slowly stripped them off, whilst gyrating from the hips
(because the ground was rather moist with juice and he didn't
    want to slip)
and the crowd quietened down because he seemed to move so well
and the serfs were all entranced (they were just as loud as a pipistrelle).

And while Gogol did his thing (and quite frankly did his stuff)
the soldiers from the Tsar had more than time enough
to pacify the peasants by beating them to a pulp
and shooting all the ringleaders and then huffing in a sulk
as Nicko pulled his trousers up and went back to the Tsar,
who said 'With a talent like that my son you're bound to go far.'
And Gogol sold two more stories that very same night,
and he knew with fans like he had, well, everything would be all right –

and it was no more go-go bars for Nikolai Gogol
no more watching sweaty men who've merely come to ogle
Nikolai Gogol.

Testimony Of A Mediaeval Monk

I'll illustrate a manuscript;
then I'll sweep the floor a bit.

The Man Whose Bed Was A House

One night, when the moon was merely a sliver of its original splendour, two burglars, who'd been out robbing in the next street along, dropped something out of one of their sacks as they ran away from the police. And what they dropped was a house. A particularly small house, not so small as you couldn't fit inside, but yet not really big enough for you to live in with a family and pets. In fact a cat might feel particularly hard done by during the measuring phase. Anyway, this house fell to the ground in an alleyway between two ordinary houses. It fitted very snugly in place, touching the walls on either side. In their haste to catch the burglars the two police officers in pursuit opened the front door, ran through the house and closed the back door after them as they continued their chase. They eventually caught up with the burglars a little later on that night and gave them a stern talking to, but neither officer remembered the little house. No one reported it missing and no one handed it in to the lost property office at the local railway station. So it stayed where it was.

Further up the street from the newly filled-in alleyway Mr and Mrs Smith were having a row. From the shouting that leaked through the walls it seemed that he'd just trod dirt into the carpet and she'd changed the channel on the television just as his programme was getting interesting. Although it could have been that he'd changed the channel just as her programme got to the good bit and she'd filled the airing cupboard up with jam again. Either way it was their thirty-fourth row that week and enough seemed to be enough.

'Mr Smith,' said Mrs Smith, 'I've had it up to there,' she pointed at a nearby church steeple, 'With your contrariness and obfuscation, either you leave this house immediately or I'll fetch the frying pan round the back of your head.' Mr Smith, being a man of undeniably common sense, packed a small suitcase with several pairs of pyjamas, his toothbrush, his glasses case and left.

He thought to himself, as he walked down the street, how he didn't have anywhere to go. His parents were visiting each other in a different town, for instance Guildford, and his only real friend was his wife, Mrs Smith. As he wandered he whistled an annoying air and swung his suitcase from left to right with unlikely freedom when suddenly he stopped. There in front of him was a little house. Not too far from the home he'd just left, which was handy because it was dark out now. In the pale glint of starlight he tried the door handle. It opened and Mr Smith went in.

The next morning the sun rose, which was, on the whole a good thing, because if it hadn't no one would have known it was the morning and waking up at, say, half past nine would have looked at their watches or alarm clocks and then looked out of the window and noticing that it was still dark would assume that the sky was right to still be so dark and that their watches and clocks were wrong to be reading so late. Nature, it seems natural to assume, is more reliable than artifice. And so they'd then go back to bed and nothing would get done, shops wouldn't open and school wouldn't start. So, as is usual, the sun rose and daylight trickled into Mr Smith's somnamulent eyes.

He'd spent the night in the little house, sat up against one of the walls, in a clean pair of pyjamas, and tried to sleep. He had managed it only very badly and in the morning looked a little scruffy, un-ironed and unshaved. Looking around he took in his surroundings. Two doors. Two windows. A nice ceiling, with a light hanging from it which connected to a light-switch just beside the front door. If he stood up and stretched his arms out to either side he could very nearly touch both walls at the same time. The front and back walls were only a little further apart than that. The cats in the earlier description were right to be worried for their safety, thought Mr Smith. He opened the front door and stepped yawning onto the pavement.

Mr Smith had his breakfast and used the lavatory and bathroom at Mrs Smith's house while she was out at work. He washed up his plate and bowl and put them on the draining board before using the telephone. He left 20p on the table for the cost of the call. He phoned a bedding shop who agreed to sell him bedding. Very shortly they sent their man round to measure Mr Smith's small house and calculate the cost and that very same afternoon they delivered his wall-to-wall mattress.

Mrs Smith knew where Mr Smith was and asked the postman to deliver his post direct to him and even leant him her sewing machine when he wanted to make curtains. As she walked past his little house each morning on her way to work she would note, without showing too much interest, any small changes he had made to the look of the place. She liked the petunias that will be mentioned in a moment and noted the small sampler pots of paint that appeared in his dustbin. Sometimes at night she would pretend to walk a dog past the little house in order, perhaps, to try to hear what channel he was watching on the television. But Mr Smith didn't have a television. And Mrs Smith didn't have a dog.

Each night he'd sleep on his mattress, tucked up under a huge thick duvet and each morning he'd eat and wash at Mrs Smith's house. Sometimes he bumped his head by bouncing too high in his house-bed and sometimes he bounced right out of one of the windows, but mostly, when at home, he just lay down. Very quickly he grew to love his house-bed very much and made some curtains and outside his little back door he set a pot of blue petunias. His house became a personal project, taking up much of his time. In some way he felt any improvement he made to it was an improvement he made to himself. Sometimes he thought about Mrs Smith and wondered what she was doing and once, when in her house, after performing his daily ablutions, he looked inside the Radio Times to see if she'd circled any particular programmes. But she hadn't.

One evening, probably a Friday, Mr and Mrs Smith realised they didn't like being alone all the time and so decided to watch television together. They agreed to watch a programme neither of them liked so as to avoid any channel changing conflicts. Sitting on the settee Mr Smith held Mrs Smith's hand gingerly and Mrs Smith held Mr Smith's other hand shyly and they both felt quite happy, although a little bored by the television. Later on they had a small argument about whose turn it was to polish the goldfish and so they stopped holding hands. But a bridge had been sketched and they knew that they still sort of liked each other.

Over the next few weeks they worked on their friendship. Sometimes Mrs Smith would visit Mr Smith's little house and would lie down on the bed next to him and look up at the ceiling. Mr Smith, you see, had not been idle in his house-bed. He had painted the ceiling a beautiful deep blue, like the night sky, and over in one corner was the moon and across the centre was the Milky Way and if you looked very carefully you could make out individual stars and if you knew the names of the constellations you'd be able to say them out loud and Mr Smith would nod at you and say, 'Yes, that's Cassiopeia,' assuming that was the constellation you'd noted.

At other times Mr or Mrs Smith would bring a neighbour into the little house-bed, say Mrs Jones for instance, and they'd stare up at the sky-ceiling and drift off in a strange sort of light slumber. It was deliciously refreshing, drifting in the house-bed. If the windows were left open you would feel the cool breeze across your face as you floated somewhere in Mr Smith's space. It was a truly most lovely place. When someone stepped on the mattress-floor at one side of the house-bed gentle undulations, like small hugging waves, would roll underneath the sleepers and dreamers and they'd murmur to themselves like the sea, while from far above ancient starlight would shower down on them.

The word did not take long to get around the street that if you were tired or upset or anxious about something then an afternoon in Mr

Smith's house-bed would be just the thing to soothe, calm or relax you. And Mr Smith was often happy to allow up to four or five people to relax in his house-bed at any one time, for although it was quite a small house it was quite a large bed. He never charged an entrance fee and often left the door unlocked.

Children would come home from school and ask Mr Smith if they could play astronauts in his house-bed and if no one was catching forty or fifty winks in there Mr Smith would open the door and turn down the gravity.

At night Mr Smith would sit with a torch doing the crossword in his paper, listening to the distant trains shuffling along their tracks, going to other towns, to other cities where, perhaps, other men sat in their own house-beds doing crosswords. He felt happy. Later on he'd lie back and open the curtains, switch off his torch and drift away with the real stars winking at him from their immense height.

One Friday evening Mr and Mrs Smith were watching television together in Mrs Smith's house. This had become something of a pleasant ritual recently, and they seemed to argue less. Mrs Smith put it down to the fact that Mr Smith had found his calling in helping people with his house-bed and she could tell he was satisfied inside himself. Mr Smith put it down to the fact that Mrs Smith didn't want to watch so much rubbish on the television any more. Whatever the cause and whatever the reason, everyone had noticed the improvement and the whole street had become a warmer and happier place.

The local news was on the television and Mr and Mrs Smith were watching with interest an article about the local zoo. Several elephants, it appeared, had escaped from the enclosure in which they lived and were now rampaging, hungrily and without adequate forethought, through the town. At this very moment they heard a crash and a bang and a thump and a thud and a trumpet and another crash from outside. Mrs Smith jumped up and grabbed her coat, ready to go head for the door. On the television a reporter and cameraman had just caught up with one of the runaway elephants and Mr Smith watched as his little house came into view and vanished beneath the four thick grey legs. Mrs Smith stood by the front door, her hand on the handle as an elephant-shaped shadow passed by the house, shaking the floor and rattling the teapot as it went. Mr Smith did not get up from the settee. They looked at each other quietly. She sat back down beside him and put her arm around his shoulder. She said he could stay the night in her house. He thanked her.

The next morning Mr Smith looked at the wreckage that had been, just a day before, his little house. His little house-bed. The dust was settling on the top and it all seemed frightfully grey and a bit of a mess. He picked a piece of plaster up and turning it over in his hands found that it was the crescent moon that had been in the sky when he first found his little house. He sat down and took off his glasses. With his handkerchief he mopped his eyes and blew his nose. He felt all hollowed out inside. Mrs Smith came and sat beside him and held his hand.

Later on that morning a dustcart from the council came round and men scooped up all the broken bits of house and took them away to the dump, leaving the alleyway open and unobstructed once more, except for one small pot of blue petunias. The neighbours watched in silence as the dustcart drove off, knowing that something special was lost to them all, because Mr Smith's house-bed had in a way become their house-bed too.

Mr Smith stared at the empty space in the mouth of the alleyway and cried until he had little left to cry. His eyes became dry and red and his nose was sore. His arms felt heavy with sorrow and he would have slumped down on the pavement had Mrs Smith not, at that moment, led him back to their old, normal-sized, house and made him a cup of tea.

Even that very morning, as he turned his back on the alleyway, he knew, in his head, that house-beds are all very well and good, but that they cannot really be expected to last forever, because otherwise what it is that is special about them would become simply commonplace.

In Mr Smith's memory what was special will, instead, become more special with each passing day and year. And indeed as the years pass by Mr Smith will eventually come to understand all this with his heart as well, for hearts aren't as easily lost as they may sometimes seem, although, understandably, that day of understanding may well be a long time coming.

Weather Dialogue

Father: Son, whether it's leather weather
  or feather weather
  it's weather we'll weather together.

Son: Father, I'd rather not tether together
  for I'm off to feather the nether of Heather.